FINANCIALS4GENZ

How To Set Yourself Up With A Firm Financial Foundation

CASEY L WILLIAMS

DEDICATION

I want to dedicate this book to my family. Thank you for your love, support, and prayers.

CONTENTS

INTRODUCTION

U p to this point in your life, your financial security was closely knitted to that of your parents – and rightly so. But if you are now finishing up high school or going into your final year in college, you are quickly going to realize that your piggy bank days are over. I know you have had the speech before *"blah blah, you need to be responsible, blah blah, money doesn't grow on trees."* Annoying, right?

I know what you are saying. *"My parents don't know what they are talking about. They've never lived. My time and their time are different."* Well…in some ways, you are right. Your parents did not grow up with Facebook, Twitter, Snapchat or the million and one other social media and gadget centered activities that you cannot imagine your life without. Yes, your parents spent their childhood without a computer and maybe even God forbid – television. But listen, money management has been with us forever and the financial concepts of the 1950s are the same for today and tomorrow. Your parents were once in high school, may have gone to college, maintained a full-time job, and financially provided for you. You will have to do the same.

So, ask yourself *"how did mom do it?"* *"How did dad make sure all the bills were paid?"* These were things you never had to think about as a child living under their roof. You never had to worry about how many hours your parents had to work to get you that Christmas gift or plan that princess sweet sixteen party. The truth is you never had to wonder about the financial planning that Auntie Sue or Uncle John had to go through in order to invest in your piggy bank. All you know is that when you needed something, you asked…and most of the time you got it.

Here is something to think about. Being old

prevents your parents from understanding the world in which you live; but their age gives them an advantage you don't have – life experiences. Their nagging is a representation of their love for you and a warning to not make the same mistakes that they did as they stepped into their financial responsibilities. But trust me, they know what they are talking about, and if you don't want to listen to them – no problem. Continue reading this book, or just continue living.

As you progress through high school or college, life is going to hit you with huge financial responsibilities. There is no delete button and unfortunately, bills will not just disappear like snapchats. The real-world approaches and the best tool you have is information.

When you tally up your bills and look at your first paycheck, you are going to need to have some budget knowledge to help you. When you want to buy your first car, information about what to expect and how to manage that financial acquisition is going to come in handy. When you meet your significant other and you decide to get married and have a family, financial education is going to be your shield. When those times come – and trust me they will – you are going to wish you listened to your parents and that you continued to read this book.

It is time for a reality check! It is time to say goodbye to your piggy bank years and the days of allowances. Those were the good ol' days. Those were the days when you lived at home with your parents – who paid for everything. Your piggy bank years left you with little or no financial responsibility to provide the things you need – clothes, shelter, food, etc. In the piggy bank years, there were no worries about money or bills.

As you got older, your parents started to give you some responsibilities – aka chores. Additionally, you may have had a pet. This is the closest you were going to get to playing mommy or daddy. You would have to feed the pet, give it water, and see to its well-being. If you are an older sibling, you may have taken on the role of babysitting. And then something great started to happen – you started to get an allowance. Now you had the power to buy stuff and do things, and God forbid - save!

I remember when I was in high school and started to get an allowance. We lived on a farm and I would get $60 per month. I thought *"great I have my own money to do whatever I want!"* Oh! But there was a catch. My parents bought one pair of shoes for school and one pair of jeans. Everything else I had to buy out of my allowance. It was an early start to financial responsibility and I don't think I liked it at first. But I remember the valuable lessons it taught me and I'll never forget them.

It is important to have that money talk early and frequently. Without this discussion, you might get stuck in the piggy bank years and the big bank phase will be hard to manage. The objective is not to nag you or bore you to death with a serious topic. The goal is to prepare you for life, allowing you to understand money, how to manage, and respect it. You can be financially responsible and still have fun.

How you deal with money starts in your mind, not in your wallet. If it's a stressor for you to always wish you had more, you spend more than you earn, or you get into deep debt, you have money blocks.

The truth is our view of money starts very early in life, age 0-7 is when we first learn about money. So, this means our money story is often structured by our parents. If your parents struggled with their finances, you have a greater tendency to as well unless you are aware of it and make changes to correct it. The earlier you realize this and take action, the better your financial story will be.

The adults that I meet that are struggling are often the author of their own fate, because they never had that money talk early in life or if they did, they allowed it to go in one ear and out the other; sound familiar? They get out into the working world, start to get some real money, but with no proper money management, they live from paycheck to paycheck. They get into "bad" debt and without the knowledge or skills to get their finances in order they continue down a path to bankruptcy. Transitioning to the big bank is no joke!

In this book, you will learn about:

1. Financing college
2. Dealing with the financial responsibilities of a first job
3. Paying for your wedding
4. How to acquire assets and manage debts
5. Dealing with the rainy days

My hope is that at the end of this book, you will be equipped with the knowledge you need to step in your financially independent years confident and ready for life.

CHAPTER ONE

FINANCING COLLEGE

Prior to college, the largest expense you probably incurred was going to the prom, or if you had a summer or part-time job, then buying your first car. Going to college is without a doubt a great investment in your future. It is also incredibly expensive if you don't have a plan. If you are currently looking at your options for college, this chapter is going to really help you. The average American lives from paycheck to paycheck, so unless you come from a wealthy family with a college fund, your parents are pulling out their hair right now!

The economic cost of a college education is not cheap. One-year tuition at a private college can run you more than $33,000. If you plan on attending a public college in your state, then you will have to fork out almost $10,000 per year and if out of state then you are looking at approximately $25,000 per year.

So, what are your options? It would be nice if you could find a rich uncle or aunt who has no plans of having kids – then jackpot! But for the rest of us, here are the options to finance all or part of your college education:

1. Grants;
2. Scholarships; and
3. Loans.

Grants

Grants and scholarships are often referred to as "gift-aid" because they represent free money that is used for financing a college education. However, the distinction between grants and scholarships is the qualifying requirements. Grants are generally need-based while scholarships are often merit-based.

Although grants are free money, if you receive one, there will be parameters to that grant. In some cases, just like with a scholarship, you may have to maintain a certain GPA. Additionally, some grants require that you be a full-time student or that you remain enrolled for a period of more than a year. It is important to understand first, nothing in life is free and that secondly, you must read the fine print. If you don't take the time to understand the parameters of the grant, you might find yourself having to pay back the money if you are in breach or being cut off mid-year.

Scholarships

A college scholarship is what we all want – right? This is why your parents urge you to do well in high school and keep up your grades – so that you can get a full scholarship to college. Which, by the way, is a win-win situation for everyone involved. Your parents don't have to pull out their hair trying to find the money to send you to college, and you don't have to spend the rest of your life paying student loans.

The most sought-after scholarships are what

are referred to as full ride scholarships. Which means that it will cost you nothing to go to school. But like grants, scholarships have parameters. These normally include maintaining certain grades or participating in a sports program. Let's say that you get a full ride scholarship to be in the band; which means that you're going to go to college with a band program, apply yourself academically, and go to practice. You will lose the scholarship if you quit the band or if your grades are bad. So, there are always parameters for a scholarship and a cost (in this case, time and hard work).

How do you go about accessing these scholarships? A good place to start is with your high school. The Guidance Counselor generally has a list of the available scholarships that you can access for college. The objective is to apply for every possible scholarship that you can get. It matters not if it is big or small because it will all add up in the end. Even if you get $250, that money could go towards buying books and that is one less thing you may have to worry about.

So, it's worth your time to apply for those scholarships. It could be some of the quickest money you will ever make.

Don't roll your eyes at me. Sounds like your parent, right? Because your parents probably told you the same thing – "apply for all of the scholarships that you possibly can apply for. You'll get something and something's better than nothing when it comes to school." They are right! Listen to them.

There are also scholarships offered by the college for enrolled students. It is, therefore, good to be in the know. If you are in high school now, go and talk with your guidance counselor and if you are in college, check out scholarship information in your student service office.

Loans

The real deal is that not everyone will get a scholarship or any other financial aid. For the majority of those seeking a college education, student loans are going to be the next best option. Loans carry a long-term commitment and even with a great job, you might find yourself paying student loans well into your forties – so get to work on those scholarships and grants.

If you can't get enough "free money" then loans can cover the balance. Generally, when someone applies for a loan, there is a requirement to start repayment the next month and interest starts to accrue immediately. However, you want a student loan, that delays repayment until after school and does not start to apply the interest until after graduation. Cool, right? But if that option is not available for you, then you will have to consider as a last resort, a loan that requires monthly payments right after approval. Which means my dear friend, you will have to get a job while going to college.

I am sure you have heard all the horror stories about student loans. I am not going to tell you that you will not have challenges with this debt (good debt, but still debt) long into your adult life. But as I mentioned in the introduction, having the information and financial education is going to make a huge difference in how you manage student loans. Since student loans have the most impact on your financial future, I am going to spend some time explaining the various elements associated with it.

If you have exhausted all your options and now you must apply for a student loan, you will have to go through an application process. Once your application is approved, do not look for a check in the mail or in your account. Oh no! The government is not stupid. The money is handed over to your school. You will have to sign documents at your school, so, that you can know that you are on the hook for this money. And then the clock starts to tick on repayment.

The good news is that a lot of times loan payments don't start until after you get out of school. Then depending on the type of loan you get; the interest may not start until after school as well.

I know you might be wondering why we are talking about interest. What's that? How does that affect the loan? And why do you need a loan where the interest does not start to accrue until after college? So, let me break it down for you. In a loan, there is a principal (the amount of money you borrow) and the interest (the add-on sum you pay in addition to the principal). The interest is what makes it worthwhile for the lender.

Let's say that you borrow $250,000 to pursue your college education. The bank or the government writes a check to your school for $250,000 and you start school. We're going to say that the loan has an interest rate of 3 percent – now that isn't the typical rate, this is just to explain it to you. The $250,000 is what is referred to as the principal – the amount of the check that was issued to the school. Generally, you get a grace period of six months after finishing school before you are expected to start paying.

What is 3% of 250,000 (I hope you were paying attention in math class…lol)? Yep, I know you just going to use your calculator! The amount is $750. So, at the end of that six months, you will owe $250,000 plus $750. You then must make your first payment. The objective is to always try to pay down the principle.

I'll use some smaller numbers to show you how it works. Let's say your first payment is $50 and you pay $2 to the principal and $48 to the interest, this is what your breakdown will look like:

	Payment	Principal	Interest	Total Interest
Month 1	$50.00	$2.00	$48.00	$48.00

Then for month two, interest is applied again, and you are on a slow boat to China to pay off this massive debt (good debt, but still debt). Below is a table to show you how far you will get in a year. Notice how the interest is most of your payment that first year?

	Payment	Principal	Interest	Total Interest
Month 1	$50.00	$2.00	$48.00	$48.00
Month 2	$50.00	$3.00	$47.00	$95.00
Month 3	$50.00	$4.00	$46.00	$141.00
Month 4	$50.00	$5.00	$45.00	$186.00
Month 5	$50.00	$6.00	$44.00	$230.00
Month 6	$50.00	$7.00	$43.00	$273.00
Month 7	$50.00	$8.00	$42.00	$315.00
Month 8	$50.00	$9.00	$41.00	$356.00
Month 9	$50.00	$10.00	$40.00	$396.00
Month 10	$50.00	$11.00	$39.00	$435.00
Month 11	$50.00	$12.00	$38.00	$473.00
Month 12	$50.00	$13.00	$37.00	$510.00

Now, if all you had to pay was a student loan, then that would be great. But there is more to life than student loans. You are going to get out of school and what's the first thing you want to do? Get your own place, right? After all, you want a taste of true freedom – no school, no parents, and money in your account. So, you rent an apartment; maybe you are prudent, and you get a roommate to share the financial burden. But after two or so years, it is time for more. Now you have found someone special and you are ready to get married and have children. So far you have been doing okay with paying all the bills, inclusive of the student loan. But then you face some financial hardship. It might be that you lose your job or incur a huge and emergency medical expense. What then?

You have options. There are forbearance and deferment. The former stops the enforcement of the debt that is due, and the latter is the act of delaying or postponing the loan payment. Now, the government or the bank are not mind-readers, so you will have to apply for either option and a determination will be made as to whether you qualify.

In a forbearance, the payments are stopped,

but the interest continues to accrue. So, it would be best to try and pay the interest. This option is best suited for when your financial situation is such that you are not able to afford the full monthly payment.

But let us say you decide to go back to school. Then a deferment might be your best option. No interest will accrue, but at the end of your studies your first loan will be added to your second loan and the cycle of payments will continue long into your adult years.

There is no real way to know how much you will pay in student loans. There are various factors at play. I know at one point my student loan monthly payment was $750. I thought that was ridiculously high, but then there were individuals paying $1,300 per month. There is no getting around it. Student loans are great because for many it is the only financial option available, but it can linger for decades. Without the right financial management, you might face true financial hardship. Oh, and forget about bankruptcy – you cannot get rid of student loans even after applying for bankruptcy.

So, my deepest apologies for the gloom and doom. But guess what? There are solutions and I want you to take note of these tips as you think about financing your college.

1. Do well in school. Your focus should be to get good grades. Ask for help and practice at home. Good grades are your best chances for a scholarship.
2. Get involved. Maybe the academics are a little challenging but getting involved in sports may open scholarship doors for you.
3. Apply for every and any (big or small) grant or scholarship.
4. If you must get a student loan, be prudent! Pay more towards your principle, as this reduces your balance for the next month's payment calculation and stay on top of your payments.
5. Get involved in your community. More and more scholarship committees are looking at what else you do outside

of school for their award recipients. They want a well-rounded student that values education, but also has other interests.

Here is the bright side – you have an education. How you choose to finance it will not negate the fact that it is one of the greatest assets you will possess, and no one can ever take your education away from you.

The tension is real to figure out how to pay to better yourself, but you are worth it. It's often the best thing you can do for yourself – it is an investment. I have multiple degrees and I would say I use my education every day, but I didn't always feel that way.

I had a job working in a restaurant while in college and I kept that job after graduation because it paid more than entry level accounting when I graduated. Let me let you in on a little secret. Money isn't everything. When you are selecting a career path, pick based on passion, not a paycheck. That may sound a little contradictory since this is a book on how to learn to manage your money, but the reality is if you are going to go to school for two to six years to invest in your knowledge and then work in that industry for the next 30-40 years, you should probably pick something you love.

CHAPTER 2

YOUR FIRST JOB

A s you exit school, whether high school or college, you will be introduced to new financial responsibility. If you are a college graduate, then you might be of the 44 million Americans with a huge student loan debt. Now although it is a debt to be repaid, it can also be viewed as an investment.

But let's say you skip college or defer it, for now, you are still going to have some new bills – rent, utilities, car payments, food etc. Welcome to the world of "growing up" – we all have bills. I know you are saying, 'I am just going to stay with mom and dad.' But mommy and daddy are going to expect you to contribute to bills – so there is no getting away from it.

Bills, Bills, and more Bills

So, let's break all those bills down:

Rent	800
Electric	200
Internet	100
Insurance	200
Car Payment	400
Gas	100
Groceries	100
Entertainment	200

Your numbers might not be the same as those in the example. Maybe you live in an area where internet is very inexpensive, but your rent is a lot higher. This will give you the idea though that living expenses for the basics add up very quickly. The trick is to know where your money is going and what it is doing for you.

At some point, you will have a bank account if you do not already. You should track each money movement, in or out, for your account. I have included a check register in the resources section of this book for you for just this purpose. If you are aware of where your money is and what it is doing for you, it will make you think twice before spending it on something foolish. This will be even more evident if you have a financial goal you are looking to achieve.

Now there is no shame in staying with parents once out of college or after getting a job after high school. In fact, it might be one of the best financial decision you make as you move into adulthood.

The reality is that it can take a lot to live on your own. When my son was in high school, he took an economics class and they were discussing whether you could live on minimum wage. The simple answer is yes, but you will do so without the standard of living that you are accustomed to at home. Staying with Mom and Dad will give you the cushion you need to start saving and pay down some of your debts.

Needs Versus Wants

Moving from getting an allowance or doing part-time gigs to receiving a regular paycheck can lead to bad decisions about spending. One of the biggest financial mistakes that you can make as you enter this time in your life is to splurge on the things you want and neglect your needs.

Financial responsibility dictates that you become cognizant of the price of the luxury items that you want in life. And not just their price tag, but also how purchasing your wants can cost you later when your needs are not being met. Remember when your Kindergarten teacher taught you about your needs and your wants; well it is time to pull out that lesson.

So, what are your needs? You need a roof over your head, clothes to wear (and not necessarily expensive name brand ones), food in your belly (and not dining out at expensive restaurants every day), and your bills (electricity, water, and gas). Yep, I know you guys are the internet generation; so yes, having internet will classify as a need.

But what is not going to be on your needs list is the greatest console for your game or the fastest internet speed available (unless it is necessary for your job!) What is not a need is having tons of television channels or a new iPhone every time it is released. Those are going to be your wants. And so, as you start out working, whether living at home with parents or being on your own, you will need to sit down and pencil out what your needs cost and how much money it will take to satisfy your wants.

With that picture in mind, you may have to shave off some of your wants because your income will not meet it. That right there is your budget. It doesn't have to be a negative feeling but does need to be realistic. I have included a budget template in the resources section of this book. With that first job, that first bank account also comes that responsibility of making sure you are tracking the money movement. I have included a bank reconciliation template in the resources section of this book for you so you can make sure you and the bank match at the end of each month.

Money Management

Your first salary will always look great. After all, you would be moving from no money to probably thousands of dollars per month. It is like giving a five-year-old $5 in a dollar store; he thinks he is rich and can buy all the toys he wants.

But you are also moving from no bills to tons of bills, debt, and the need for future planning. Do not get ahead of your self and waste your first paycheck on all the things you ever wanted. Look at your check stub each pay period. Make sure your hours and pay rate are correct. You should look at the taxes coming out of your check too.

I know it's a little depressing to see how much you pay in tax each payday, but that is a form of contributing to society. There are two things certain in life - death, and taxes.

So, what do you do with what's left after taxes? My advice is that you should live (that means paying your bills) on eighty percent of your income. What do you do with the remaining twenty percent? At least ten percent of your salary should go towards charity. It is our duty as people of society to give to the less fortunate. I don't care if you give it to a food pantry, the local Red Cross, United Way, an animal shelter, a church; find a cause that is important to you and develop a habit of donating regularly.

What you do with the next ten percent is critical. This is something that grown adults struggle with, but if you start early it will get easier. With the next ten percent of your salary open an account for saving. Be deliberate about this each paycheck; let it be the first thing you do or have it as a standing deduction every month.

The average American lives from paycheck to paycheck without any cushion in case of an emergency or if they lose their job. Your savings is going to help you deal with a health emergency, car emergency, or just in case you need some fast cash to handle a financial surprise.

Money management is something that people learn over time. Unfortunately, they don't teach enough of it in high school or college, which can lead to financial pitfalls when you get that initial paycheck.

As you start to get this nice, big, fat paycheck that you've never had before, you do not want to go out and make crazy purchases, such as buying a new car. You need to be careful with your spending as you enter into this new time in your life.

Now I am not saying that you ought to be a bore and never buy anything nice or not to go to nice places. But you want to make sure that you are striking a happy medium and that your budget can afford it.

You need to make sure that you can pay yourself first (save), bills, and then with what is leftover, you can consider the wants; taking into consideration that you must do the research and shop around to make sure that you are always making the right financial decision.

Let's take the purchase of a car as an example. This will probably be your first big ticket expense. As a first-time car buyer, you go to the dealership, look at the price tag and figure "yes I can afford that!"

But, the financial commitment to buying a car includes more than the sticker price. In addition to your monthly payment, you will have to get insurance, plus there is the cost to get tags and registration, buying gas from month to month and regular maintenance. Then there is the occasional work that must be done on the vehicle and buying tires. Cars are not cheap, and their value NEVER increases after you drive it off the lot. So, be financially prudent and do your research.

The same thing can be said about buying a house. If you happen to get a really great job straight out of college and have the capacity to buy a house or condo, remember there is more to home ownership than just the monthly mortgage payments. There is closing costs, insurance, and other professional fees associated with buying real estate. If you get past that, utilities are higher in a house (more square footage), you are now responsible for the maintenance of the home and all appliances and you lose the luxury of calling the leasing office. This is when having a savings account is going to come in quite useful.

You are going to find that budgeting is critical to your financial intelligence as you embrace your new financial responsibilities. Budgeting allows you to be more cognizant of where you're spending your money. If all you are doing is swiping a card and hoping for the best, then that isn't budgeting. You should always know how much money you have and where it is going.

So, is your money management as a colander or a funnel? If it is a colander then when you put your money in it pours out everywhere, but if it is a funnel, your money comes out at one specific point that you can control, and it is coming out in a smaller quantity than what you are pouring it. What you want is a funnel, so that you are in control. You are only able to achieve this through budgeting. Budgeting always seems like a bad word, but the truth is when done right it is an effective financial tool.

Budgeting

Budgeting can be fun, I promise. So here we go. First, make a list of all your expenses and I would list out expenses based on when they are due. Let's say that your mortgage or rent is due the first of the month and then your telephone bill is due the fifth of the month, your cable bill is due on the 10th and your car payment is due the 15th of the month – you want to list them in the order that they will be paid.

Then attach the amount of money due to each of the expenses. So how much is your rent? How much do you spend on groceries, and so forth? Now, don't forget that your budget should also include a sum for donation and for savings.

Now there are a number of ways to set up your budget, but I personally like the old-fashioned cash envelope system and here's why. When you walk up to the cash register and you swipe that card through the card reader or you tap your phone at checkout, there's no emotional attachment to that. It's the same emotion whether it's $3 or $300.

However, if you must spend dollar bills out of your envelope, there is an emotional attachment to that money because you are physically touching the money and giving it away. I try to turn it into a game – "How can I go under the budget today?" And when I do I feel like a winner.

We live in a commercial environment that encourages buying on credit, opening store cards and it is easy to get caught up in getting it now and paying for it later. When you pay for it later you might also be paying interest as well. Budgeting does not mean that you are going to be mean and tight, it just means that you understand what you have and what you spend. The more you commit to maintaining your budget, the further your money will go, and the easier it will be to make the larger investments in life – like those we will cover in the next two chapters.

CHAPTER 3

THE WEDDING DAY

I hear wedding bells! Life comes with some major events; your wedding day is one of them. It can also be a very expensive investment or debt; whichever way you want to look at it. The average cost for a wedding (the ones with a church, big dress, venue, lots of people, food, band, and all of the good stuff!) is between $25,000 and $30,000. This cost will be even more expensive depending on where you decide to tie the knot. For example, the average cost of a wedding in Manhattan is $78,000 – yep – more than your student loan debt.

So here is the thing – will all of the fancy stuff matter in the long run? After all, whether you spend $50,000 or $5,000, you will still be married. I think all that matters is the legality of the event, the rest is luxury. But for many having hundreds of people to celebrate their love and having the fancy dress and expensive flowers creates memories that their low-budget wedding may not achieve. Whatever your preference, there is an important question you must answer – "What are you willing to spend for memories?"

The Cost to Say "I Do"

I want you to remember that the wedding industry feeds on the emotions – particularly of the bride – and the price tags are set accordingly. If you isolate the feelings of what people will think and wanting to please as many people as possible, then you can really sit down with your partner and work out a realistic budget for your wedding.

Like any other big expense in your life, you cannot get away from doing some research. You need to know what professionals are involved, what services you need to have, what are the things you have to buy and how much of a financial dent is it going to make to your bank account. So here is a list to guide you with your research.

1. **Wedding venue**. This might include two venues; one for the actual ceremony and another for the reception. Generally, when the ceremony is at a church, a separate reception venue is needed. All venues have a rental cost, and, in most instances, you will be required to pay a deposit to secure the locations. The cost will vary depending on whether you are using your parents backyard versus a hotel ballroom and also whether you are hosting 50 or 500 people.

2. **Wedding officiant**. This is the person with the legal authority to marry you and your partner. Even if you get a pastor, he or she will have an officiating fee and you may be required to pay a deposit to secure the individual for your wedding day. If this person does not turn up, then there can be no wedding. Although this is the most

important service that you will need for your wedding it may very well be the cheapest expenditure in your budget.

3. **Food and drinks**. Now, this is what most of the guests will pay attention to and the price tag can vary depending on the number of courses you want and the size of your guest list. If you are having hard liquor or an open bar, you could be looking at a lot of money to feed your wedding guests. Just like any other expense, you have to pay a deposit.

4. **Wedding Attire**. In most cases, the bridal party will pay for their attire to the wedding. But the bride's wedding gown and the groom's suit will rake in thousands of dollars in your budget. Plus, you may have to pay for attire for close family members like the parents of the bride and the groom. In some instances, you may have to hire a seamstress and a tailor. Some people might push the envelope and hire a stylist.

5. **Wedding décor**. This relates to the decoration (flowers, centerpieces, floating angels etc.) This is one of those expenses that can range from $0 to tens of thousands of dollars. Most weddings will come with a theme and will require manpower and time to execute the vision- all adding to the cost.

6. **Wedding professionals**. These will include wedding planners, photographer, caterers, makeup artist, hair stylist, and the band. All of these professionals have separate prices for weddings and depending on your needs wedding professionals can eat up a lot of your wedding budget.

Now, I have not even mentioned the wedding rings and the honeymoon. Two very high-ticket items and once again will vary depending on your taste. But here is the deal, your wedding need not cost thousands of dollars, a courthouse ceremony or a private backyard wedding can be inexpensive and leave you with enough memories to last a lifetime. But whatever the choice – make sure you can afford it; really afford it!

So, after you have done the necessary research to understand what the estimated cost is for a wedding, it is time for you to sit with your future husband or wife and figure out what you both are willing to spend on the wedding.

The Wedding Talk

This discussion is going to open your eyes to the expectations of your future spouse. You will need to talk about all the areas of the wedding. Will we be inviting all of our families, even those from out of town? Are we doing indoor or outdoor? Are we renting or buying wedding attire? Do we want fake flowers or will silk flowers do? Do not assume anything, discuss everything and attach a figure to them all. This level of communication and transparency will serve you long after you are married.

Then there is another cost that you will have to discuss – life after the wedding. If you were living apart, now as husband and wife you may need to get a new place. You might have to get furniture, make a deposit, and even get a car if you were driving your parent's car before. These are some of the new expenses that will arise after the wedding and you want to make sure you are ready for them as well. You need to make sure that you have open communication between the two of you, especially when you start this planning process before you get very far because you want to make sure that the wedding budget matches the commitment and the plan.

Now that you have had the money talk, you need to know who is paying for what. The idea that the bride's family pays for the wedding is far gone from mainstream culture. So, after you know what you want and what it will cost, it is time to figure out, who will pay for what. In most cases, parents will chip in, but do not leave it up to chance, find out early what each parent can, and is willing to contribute to the wedding.

Be very realistic about what you or your spouse can afford. Your taste might be more expensive than your bank account! The higher the cost of the wedding, the more likely you will be putting most of the expenses on a credit card. This is not something I recommend, but it is a reality for many who did not save for this day or whose income cannot afford it. Now credit cards carry interest and so you might be paying for this wedding and more months and even years after the big day. You will have to pull out your financial prudence and determine what's more important – spending $20,000 on a wedding or spending that same amount for a deposit on a house?

Being financially prudent is going to be even more important if you and your spouse are in your early or mid-twenties and just starting out in life. It is not cute to have this elaborate wedding and then have to move your spouse into your parent's home because you went broke paying for a wedding you could not afford.

In most instances, the proposal will happen one year or even two before the actual day. As early as possible do the research, set a budget and agree on what that price tag will be. With at least a year ahead, you can start to save for the day. It might mean no vacations for that year, doing overtime at work, or taking on a part-time job that will go towards the wedding fund. Map out what you will need to save to meet your portion of the wedding budget and then work towards that. It might mean you have to tighten your budget for that year, but it sure beats putting it all on a credit card.

Putting on your big boy or big girl underwear and being financially responsible will pay off and you will see the benefits as you move forward in acquiring assets as a family.

CHAPTER 4

ACQUIRING ASSETS & DEBTS

You will quickly come to realize that when you have a job, life is all about paying bills. They come every month and every day you will find yourself incurring daily expenses that are central to your existence. Even when the activity is something fun – like a vacation or going to the mall – it requires money. It may initially seem like a vicious cycle of getting paid and quickly thereafter using that money to pay bills and not seeing any benefit from it all. But this is where assets come into play. Now that you have a job, you should be thinking about acquiring things that will not only improve your standard of living but also your financial standing.

Buying a Car

One of the first things you might invest in is a car. There are a lot of options when looking to buy a car and it is important you understand what they are and not just jump at the first deal you come across.

Option one is to buy the vehicle free from a loan. In this case, you are buying the vehicle outright and will have no monthly payment. Unless you just won the lottery or came into a significant amount of money, your budget will only allow you to pursue this option with an older car. The ability to exercise this option may come after months of diligent savings, but it is important that you get the help of a mechanic or someone knowledgeable about cars before you sign on the dotted line.

Option number two is the most popular option. If you are not able to save to buy a car outright, you may choose the financing option. This means that you pay a portion of the sale price upfront (referred to as a deposit) and then apply to a bank or other financial institution for them to loan you the money to pay off the balance. The person or dealership selling the car gets payment in full, you get your car, but you will have to pay monthly payments to the financial institution that provided the loan. Your loan will include the principal amount (the amount paid for the car) and interest (the cost to get the loan).

Option number three is referred to as leasing. In all the other options you are the owner of the car. However, when you lease a car the vehicle remains the property of the dealership and essentially you pay them monthly to use the car. In real terms, you are borrowing the car for a specific period of time and within the terms of the lease contract. There will be insurance restrictions as well as mileage restrictions. At the end of the lease, you have to return the vehicle to the dealership.

There are several factors that will determine which option you will pursue. You will have to look at your financial situation in each option and your transportation requirements. There is always a benefit to having a car, but the decision to buy should be pursued carefully.

When buying an older vehicle, you want to think about maintenance and upkeep of the vehicle. The amount of money you will spend on a used car in terms of maintenance will normally be less if you purchased a newer car. However, if you purchased the used car without financing, then the monthly savings from not paying a car loan is a big benefit and can be used to offset any maintenance issues you may have after purchasing the car.

It's going to be important that you carry out some research. Whether you are buying with cash, financing, or leasing, you want to put all the pros and cons on the table. Now with ride-sharing services like Uber and Lyft, people are finding that there are plenty of options when determining whether to buy a car or not. For example, if you live walking distance from home and in an area where shopping, dining, and entertainment are close by, you might find it financially prudent to just uber back and forth and rent a car for trips out of town.

Owning a car is a great freedom, but the cost to keep a car is ongoing. The big mistake that people make is that they focus on the sticker price and how much they can pay monthly and they figure "oh I can manage that!" But the reality is that there are other financial tags that come with owning and in some cases with even leasing a car.

1. License plates
2. Insurance
3. Fuel
4. Oil changes
5. Tires
6. General maintenance

Most of your monthly bills are pretty much predictable and with the right budgeting strategies, you will be able to manage your finances monthly. But there will always be emergencies, and this is the same for a car. You may get into an accident that is your fault, or one of your tires blows out on the highway. Then there are circumstances in which you are rushing to work, get into your car and it just will not start. Any of these emergencies can set you back in mechanic, towing, and other costs. So, you will want to allocate a certain amount to your savings to deal with such eventualities.

So here are my tips when buying a car:

1. Know and research your options.
2. Get a mechanic to help in your decision to buy a used car.
3. Examine your finances to see if you are able to afford a car.
4. Always have rainy day savings account to deal with unforeseen expenses.

Buying a House

The next thing on your list will be a home – nope you can't live with mom and dad for life. So, what are your options; you can rent, or you can buy. The former is a great move as a start or the best option if your job has you moving. However, when you rent, that property is not yours, while on the other hand buying is a long-term investment and a very serious one.

Just like buying a car, there is a number of additional costs associated with buying a house. Some of those expenses start before you even get the house and includes having money for a deposit, closing costs, and attorney fees. So, it goes without saying that you will need to save up for your out of pocket expenses.

More than likely you will be getting a loan to cover the balance of the purchase price and you will have to go through the mortgage application process – which is much more strenuous compared to buying a car. The bank is going to look at your work history, your income, your credit score, how responsible you've been making your payments for other things like your credit cards, your car payment, your utilities. If you're new to the work scene, you may be required to have someone to sign with you on the loan. Often that's a parent or a sibling that's been working longer and has a more established work history.

The bank looks at your credit score, which is a ranking system that they use on your payment history. The bank wants to know that you are a responsible adult and that you're going to be able to make your payments to them each month. If you are interested in knowing your credit score, you can look for a free service like Credit Karma. This site doesn't cost you to look up your score and checking your credit score on this site will not affect your score. If you have bad credit, you may have to take some time to work on your credit before being ready to buy a house.

When you are ready to go ahead with this investment, it can be an exciting time. However, the best approach is to find out what you are approved for in terms of the mortgage amount before you go house shopping. Once you know what you can afford you can start to look at properties in your budget. During your house shopping, you want to make sure that you do nothing to affect your credit score. Any downward movement in your score could affect your final mortgage approval.

Another factor you must bear in mind is the cost of owning a home. You will be making a mortgage payment for the next 15 to 30 years and unlike renting you are responsible for maintenance and everything else connected to the property. Accordingly, you must pay for insurance, property taxes, and any maintenance or repair that is needed; and trust me this will be needed. There is no luxury of calling the leasing office or a landlord, you will have to be financially ready to repair the roof if needed, fix pipes and deal with so many other unforeseen repairs of a home. On the plus side, the property is yours and all your mortgage payment and other money that you put into the house goes towards your equity.

Just like with buying a car, the loan the bank gives you for buying your house comes at a cost – interest. You want to make sure you get a fixed rate interest on your loan because if you get a variable rate, that means that your rate can change at any time depending on the market. You may find yourself owing more than what the house is valued if interest rates balloon in a variable interest rate loan.

Once you have a home, paying your mortgage should be your top priority every month. However, it is also good to pay more than what is expected to reduce the length of the loan. However, any payment above and beyond the monthly mortgage payment should be applied to the principal, which will make life better for you in the long run.

In the first few years, as you are paying your mortgage, you will probably not have equity in the property. This simply means that what you owe is equal to or more than the value of the house. But as you continue to pay, how much you owe to the bank will decrease over time and you will begin to have equity in the home. This means that you will owe less than the value of the house. This equity can be used to get further loans to do improvement on the property or any other financial need you may have as you progress in life. By far having a home can be a great asset to pursue as you start to build a successful future...but are you ready?

There are a couple of things to consider if you are ready to purchase a home. You have the emotional side – Are you ready to be on your own? You may feel so ready to leave your parent's nest and start to build a home for yourself. Being emotionally ready includes an understanding that there is no going back to mommy or daddy; you are taking a huge step to independence. You are going to find that being emotionally ready is the easy part of it. There are plenty of people who want to leave their parent's home or stop renting, but they can't. Although they are emotionally ready, they may not be financially ready to make that move.

Now being ready financially is a whole different ballgame. To begin with, you would need to have approximately 20 to 30 percent of the purchase price of the house as a deposit. This money is due upfront and so unless you just inherited some serious cash or won the lottery, you will have to save towards this goal.

Then there are taxes, insurance and the ongoing upkeep and maintenance and utilities and all the pieces that go with it. Buying a house is not cheap and maintaining it is equally expensive.

While acquiring a home may seem like a great idea, you don't want to strain yourself financially which can, in the long run, stress you out emotionally. So, you want to make sure you save the money needed for a deposit and closing cost. In addition to that, you may need to purchase certain appliances and even furniture. On a monthly basis, you may want to call in someone to do landscape plus having a handyman on call in case of emergency repairs. You want to make sure that your budget can handle the recurring expenses and that your savings can manage the emergencies from time to time.

While both a car and a house are often

necessary, they are not assets in the sense that they make money for you. Your house will hold some resale value, so on your balance sheet or your financial portfolio, it's considered an asset, but for this discussion, your house you live in and your car are not assets because they don't pay you. They add to your debt.

Debt Acquisition

So, let's talk about debt. There are different types of debt. A lot of times when individuals think about debt it is often in a negative way. However, there is good debt and then there is bad debt. One good debt is that of a loan to purchase a house. This is considered a good debt because if you are going to go into debt you want it to be for an asset that appreciates in value. This is the opposite of a car, which loses its value the day you drive it off the lot.

One of the easiest debts to incur and one that is not so good is credit card debt. With this debt, you can get into trouble really quick. Now, that's not to say that all credit cards are bad but only if you're diligent enough to pay off the balance of the card every month. A credit card is an excellent tool to use for cash financing or what is referred to as cash flow. But if you carry a balance, then you pay interest and that can get very costly very quickly.

Debt Management

Whether you consider the debt to be good, bad or necessary, everything will come down to how you manage your debt. Even though a mortgage is a good debt, if you budget poorly and fall behind on payments, then that debt is now…not so good anymore. When deciding on any debt you must first consider whether you can afford the monthly payment, but you must also look at the long-term factors associated with the debt.

Here's a good example. Let's say that you buy a house and you're paying interest and it's not simple interest. So, the bank makes out pretty good the first seven years or so as a significant portion of your payment is going to the interest and the principal is hardly moving. After that, your payments start to make a dent in the principal and you are finally making headway. But then the bank calls you and offers you a "special" and it is appealing – you could pay off credit cards or other debts with this new loan. However, here's the deal, the bank gets to start that loan over again and you're going to pay that higher interest the first seven years of that loan. So always think long term with all loans.

The other factor in debt management is your monthly payment. It is easy to just pay the minimum monthly payment on the credit card or the exact amount of the car loan each month, but that's not always the best approach. You want to pay more than the minimum amount. When you do so, you should always instruct your bank or lender that the excess payment should go to the principal. This approach which sees your loan repayment going faster than just paying the minimum monthly payment.

The other important aspect of debt

management is doing your research. Making sure you understand that there is more to a debt than the monthly payments. For a car, there is gas, insurance, licensing, and maintenance. Then there are the emergencies that might pop up from time to time. The same for buying a house, there are closing cost, the cost of appliances and the on-going cost to maintain a property.

Now I want to share with you the best practices for debt management. Despite our best intentions, some of us will get into serious debt; but the good news is that you can dig yourself out of it. So here you go:

1. First of all, make a list of all the debts. Next to each item write the total amount owed, how much is the monthly payment and the interest rate.
2. Your next goal is pay off the smallest bill on the list. You do this by paying a little bit more than the minimum balance on that specific bill, while still paying the minimum on the others.

3. Once you have completed the smallest debt you apply that extra that was being paid for the previous bill to the next lowest bill until it is paid off...and so on.

Now here's the kicker -while you are in the process of paying down your debt, don't go acquire new debt. During this process try to find spaces in your budget that could do with a little cutting. Such as cable TV, going to the movies, eating out. When your debts are managing you as opposed to the other way around, you may have to get a little uncomfortable in order to fix it. It will not happen overnight. In most cases you would have gotten into debt mess over time – so be patient but be disciplined.

Be Disciplined

So how are you going to stay disciplined? Write down your financial desire. Maybe it is to be in a position to go on vacation or buy a new car. Whatever it is...write it down. Every time you get frustrated and want to deviate from your budget, go back to the why.

You are going to notice that in your attempt to acquire assets in life and a better standard of living, you end up getting into debt. There is nothing inherently wrong with debt – after all, that's how you will more than likely buy a car or a home. The issue is how you go about managing the entire process so that you don't end up with bad credit or filing for bankruptcy.

Now that we have covered the debt side, let's talk about the asset side, which is way more fun. Assets are things that make you money. Rich people buy assets that buy them stuff, while average people buy stuff.

Let's say you want to buy a motorcycle. Now you can save and buy it and then your ongoing costs are fuel, insurance, plates, and maintenance so it's clear it's costing you even after you own it. What if I told you there was a way you get a motorcycle without having to pay for the ongoing expenses? I have good news, there is. Buy an asset and let the asset pay the expenses for you.

One of the easiest assets to purchase is a rental home. This is an asset because it pays you every month. There are a few positives to having a rental property. One, it saves you on taxes. Rentals are considered passive income, so they sort of act like a business on your taxes. That means you get to deduct some normal expenses that you already have on your taxes to save even more money, like a portion of your cell phone, the maintenance on your rental. When you replace a ceiling fan in your own house, you can't deduct that on your taxes, but in a rental, it's considered maintenance expense, which is deductible.

So, you make money each month on your rental and you let the profits from your investment pay for your fun things, like that motorcycle you have always wanted.

There are some risks in rentals too, I don't want to paint a rosy picture for you when it comes to investments, there is always a risk. The investments you want to look into are the ones that the rewards outweigh the risks.

The act of having a rental that gives you income each month is called a stream of income. This is added to your job, so now you have two streams of income. Your paycheck, and your rental. To build a true firm financial foundation, you want multiple streams of income. The experts say seven is the goal for true wealth. What else can you do to have a stream of income? Some start a side business. Maybe you want to dabble in a network marketing company. Maybe you have the knack for buying and selling investment stocks and bonds. The possibilities are endless when it comes to streams of income.

CHAPTER 5

ARE YOU READY FOR RAINY DAYS?

L ife is not always a bed of rose and sunshine all the time. Even with the best intentions and financial planning, you will encounter some rainy days – unplanned events that significantly undermine your financial stability.

Pop-up Expenses

So, imagine you are on vacation in the Bahamas with the family and your son breaks his leg on the last day of your trip. Suddenly your trip turns into a financial nightmare. You will be faced with medical bills plus the cost to change your plane tickets and extra nights at the hotel. You would also incur extra transportation cost to travel back and forth to the hospital and maybe even babysitting fees for your other children.

Then there are the rainy days that happen right at home. Sickness, a car not starting, a blown tire, job loss, and sudden death are all things that can "rain on your parade." It is all part of life; if you have never experienced it…just keep living and you will soon enough.

Since these events are unplanned and for the most part unwanted, how do you make sure that you are ready for them? It is important to have savings sufficient to cover six to eight months of your household salary. This may seem like a lot, but this will come in handy when surprise events like job loss or health emergencies face you and your family. This saving account should be held separate from your main account and there should be rules as to how it's funding will be used and replenished.

Insurance Policies

Outside of having a savings account, it is important to secure insurance policies that will protect your assets and your family on rainy days. Insurance for houses and cars are almost mandatory. But in addition to that, you will need to consider health insurance for your family to brace the cost of getting health services. Additionally, there is a need to pursue life insurances, and even funeral benefits to provide peace of mind in the case of death in the family.

Nobody likes to talk about the bad things that can happen in life. But unfortunately living in ignorance and lack of preparation can significantly affect your finances.

One way to protect yourself in addition to multiple streams of income is with life insurance. The list of kinds of insurance is as long as my arm, but I'll give you the main points here.

There are three main types of life insurance - Term, whole, and universal. All three have a death benefit. This is the amount of coverage you are purchasing. When you pass away, your beneficiary (living family members) get this money. They can choose to take this as a lump sum of money or have it in yearly deposits depending on the terms of the policy.

Another common theme about life insurance is the earlier you purchase it in life, the less expensive it is. If you purchase life insurance for your children when they are babies, it's less than $50 a year. When you get to be an adult, its more than $50 a month.

Term is just that, a term life policy. It gives protection for a price for the length of the policy. There are no other benefits to a term policy than that. The purpose would be if you take on an extra debt load and you want your family to be covered in case something happens to you while you have that loan. An example would be a home loan. You can take out a term policy that would provide extra benefits to your spouse and family in case something happens to you while you are paying off that home mortgage loan.

The opposite extreme to the term policy is the whole life policy. This has cash value and builds the entire time you have the policy and often you can live on the benefits long after the policy is paid in full when you are older. This is the least expensive from an overall view because it is worth something even after you quit paying for it.

The middle of the road, which is the most affordable monthly if you're looking to purchase insurance later in life is the universal life policy. This gives you some benefits like the whole life policy but isn't the entire suite, which is why it's more affordable.

Let me explain the whole cash value concept. When you take out a life insurance policy you pay a monthly price, which is called a premium, in exchange for a death benefit value. In the case of a whole life or universal life policy, the extra money that you pay goes into an account and your policy has a cash value of whatever the account has in it. In most cases, you can only borrow up to half of the cash value.

The nice part about a whole or universal life policy is that you can borrow from yourself should you ever need that money. There is a cost to do this, so it's not as favorable as having money in savings, but better than borrowing from a bank and you probably are not going to turn your own request down when you are in an emergency and need the money.

CONCLUSION

Ok, it's time to see how you measure up.

1. What is your yearly income?

   _____

2. What is 10% of your yearly income?

   _____

3. How much is half of your yearly income?

   _____

4. Did you open a savings account that you're calling your 'rainy day' fund?

   _____

5. Do you know how much you're supposed to be putting towards that account? I'll give you a little hint, six to eight months of your income.

---

6. The next thing that you should have done is decided on a charity that you will support. Which charity are you going to select to start?

---

7. Your next goal is to create your financial plan, also known as a budget. There is a template in the references section of this book.

8. The next thing on your list is having a checking account? I have two checking accounts that I use, one for our fun things and one for our bills. How much are you going to put in each account out of your paycheck?

---

9. Do you have life insurance for yourself, your spouse, or children? As you have children in life, you will want to get life insurance for them too. Which kind will you choose? How much do you need in a death benefit?

_____

10. After you have paid down your debts, open a second savings account and start putting money in there. Put it on your budget spreadsheet so that you have it and you can track it. How much is your goal to put in your second savings account?

_____

_____

11. What is your reward for meeting this financial goal of yours?

_____

_____

From time to time, you will need to redo your financial plan. I make a new financial plan the first of every year and I revisit it each June...because life changes. You're going to have bills today that you didn't have six months ago, and in two years you'll have all kinds of different bills that you don't have today. This will also allow, you to see progress and that will help give you the motivation to keep going. So, you'll want to make sure that you can update and change that budget as you see fit.

As you move forward to enjoy your new found financial freedom, here are some financial lessons and wisdom I want to share with you.

- ✓ Investing in yourself is always a good thing.

- ✓ Set financial goals for yourself. That gives you something to reach toward.

- ✓ Reward yourself when you reach those goals. There are rewards that will not break the bank. Maybe you choose to save $40 out of each paycheck for 6 months and then you take the family out for a nice dinner.

✓ People willing to skimp on the luxuries to meet financial goals will enjoy those luxuries later when they are not a stress on the budget so much more.

RESOURCES

Budget Template:

Due	Bills	Cur Amt	Jan pd	Feb pd	Mar pd	April pd	May pd	June pd	July pd	Aug pd	Sept pd	Oct pd	Nov pd	Dec pd
1	Savings													
1	Tithe													
	Rent													
	Electric													
	Insurance													
	Car Pmt													
	Gas													
	Groceries													
	Internet													

Check Register

Item	Date	Description/Purpose	Out	In	Total

Checkbook Reconciliation:

CheckBook Balancing Worksheet

Date

Account Balance Online as of today

Deposits Outstanding

Total Deposits

Check/Debit Card Items Outstanding

Total Checks Outstanding

Ending Balance of Checkbook Register

ABOUT THE AUTHOR

Casey L. Williams is an accountant serving clients across the United States. She recently left the corporate world to follow her passion to help others enjoy a financially stress-free lifestyle. While she is building her accounting firm, she speaks on the health benefits of a solid financial foundation.

Before starting her own business, Casey worked in public accounting, bookkeeping, payroll, and tax. Prior to that, she worked in a consulting company assisting clients on the benefits of implementing processes and procedures. Her credentials include an Associate in Accounting from International Business College in Ft Wayne, IN, and a bachelor's and master's in business administration from Indiana Wesleyan University. She is also a Quickbooks Pro Advisor. Continuing education is her form of self-care. A holistic, balanced life creates a better version of health, wealth, and happiness.

Ms. Williams is married with four children and lives in Northwest Indiana. Outside of work, she enjoys various activities such as volunteering at the local reading center and watching her children in their many endeavors.

CONNECT WITH CASEY
EMAIL: casey@caseylwilliams.com
WEBSITE: Financials4GenZ.com